Self Master

HTML CSS Javascript

YANG HU

Simple is the beginning of wisdom. From the essence of practice, this book to briefly explain the concept about HTML CSS and Javascript programming.

http://en.verejava.com

Copyright © 2019 Yang Hu

All rights reserved.

ISBN: 9781078285230

CONTENTS

First Web Page

HTML is a series of tags on a web page that format the display.

1. Create a FirstWebPage.html file with Notepad or anther Editor and open it in your browser to see the webpage

<html>: tag tells the browser that this is an HTML document.
<title>: tag it defines the title of the document.
<body>: tag defines the document's body.

\<div\> CSS Box

1. Create a Box.html file and open it in your browser to see the webpage

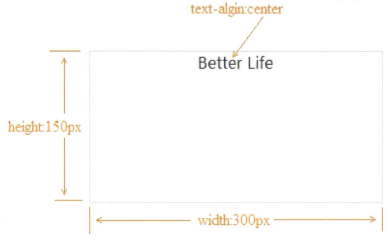

\<div\>: html tag defines a division or a section in an HTML document.

\<style\>: setting the style of an HTML element.

.class selector: css selects elements with a specific class attribute.

border: CSS properties allow you to specify the style, width, and color of an element's border.

Color: (red:#ff0000, green:#00ff00, blue:#0000ff, grey:#cccccc)

text-align: CSS properties specifies the horizontal alignment of text (left, center, right)

```
<!DOCTYPE HTML>
<html>
<head>
<title>Border</title>
   <style>
     .box{
        border:1px solid #cccccc;
        width:300px;
        height:150px;
        text-align:center;
     }
   </style>
</head>
 <body>
   <div class="box">
     Better Life
   </div>
 </body>
</html>
```

2. defines the radius of the div's corners.

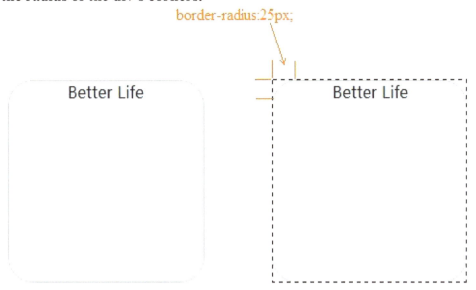

border-radius: CSS3 property defines the radius of the element's corners.

```
<style>
  .box{
    border:1px solid #cccccc;
    width:300px;
    height:150px;
    text-align:center;
    border-radius:25px;
  }
</style>

<div class="box">
  Better Life
</div>
```

3. defines the shadows of the div's box.

box-shadow: CSS3 property attaches one or more shadows to an element.

```
<style>
  .box{
    border:1px solid #cccccc;
    width:200px;
    height:200px;
    text-align:center;
    border-radius:25px;
    box-shadow: 0px 0px 5px #888888;
  }
</style>

<div class="box">
  Better Life
</div>
```

4. defines the shadows of the div's box.

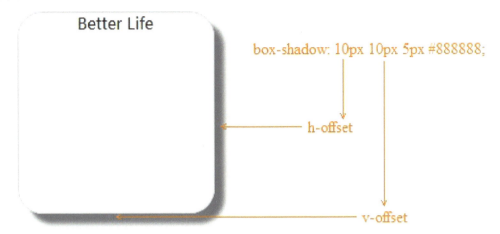

box-shadow: CSS3 property attaches one or more shadows to an element.
h-offset: The horizontal offset of the shadow.
v-offset: The vertical offset of the shadow.

```
<style>
   .box{
      border:1px solid #cccccc;
      width:200px;
      height:200px;
      text-align:center;
      border-radius:25px;
      box-shadow: 10px 10px 5px #888888;
   }
</style>

<div class="box">
   Better Life
</div>
```

5. defines the background color of the div's box.

background-color: CSS property define the color of background.
font-size:24px; CSS property define the size of font.
color:#ffffff; CSS property define the color of font.

```
<style>
  .box{
    border:1px solid #cccccc;
    width:200px;
    height:200px;
    text-align:center;
    border-radius:8px;
    background-color:#ff0000;
    font-size:24px;
    color:#ffffff;
  }
</style>

<div class="box">
  Better Life
</div>
```

6. defines the absolute position of the div's box.

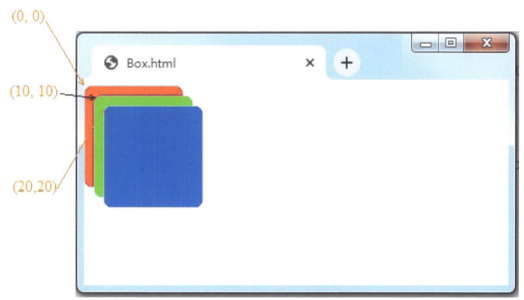

position:absolute; the element is positioned absolutely to its first positioned parent.
top: offset; CSS property defines the top position of an element.
left: offset; CSS property defines the left position of an element.

```
<style>
  .redBox{
    border:1px solid #cccccc;
    width:100px;
    height:100px;
    border-radius:8px;
    background-color:#ff0000;
    position:absolute;
    top:0px;
    left:0px;
  }
  .greenBox{
    border:1px solid #cccccc;
    width:100px;
    height:100px;
    border-radius:8px;
    background-color:#00ff00;
    position:absolute;
    top:10px;
    left:10px;
  }
```

```css
    .blueBox{
        border:1px solid #cccccc;
        width:100px;
        height:100px;
        border-radius:8px;
        background-color:#0000ff;
        position:absolute;
        top:20px;
        left:20px;
    }
</style>

<div class="redBox">

</div>
<div class="greenBox">

</div>
<div class="blueBox">

</div>
```

7. defines the relative position of the div's box.

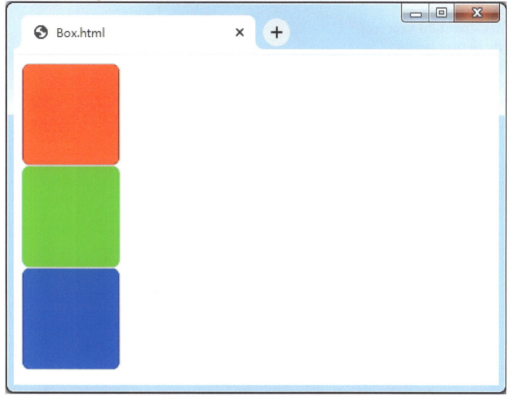

position:relative; the element is positioned relative to its normal position.

```
<style>
  .redBox{
    border:1px solid #cccccc;
    width:100px;
    height:100px;
    border-radius:8px;
    background-color:#ff0000;
    position:relative;
  }
  .greenBox{
    border:1px solid #cccccc;
    width:100px;
    height:100px;
    border-radius:8px;
    background-color:#00ff00;
    position:relative;
  }
```

```css
    .blueBox{
        border:1px solid #cccccc;
        width:100px;
        height:100px;
        border-radius:8px;
        background-color:#0000ff;
        position:relative;
    }
</style>

<div class="redBox">

</div>
<div class="greenBox">

</div>
<div class="blueBox">

</div>
```

8. defines space around an element's content, outside of the div's box.

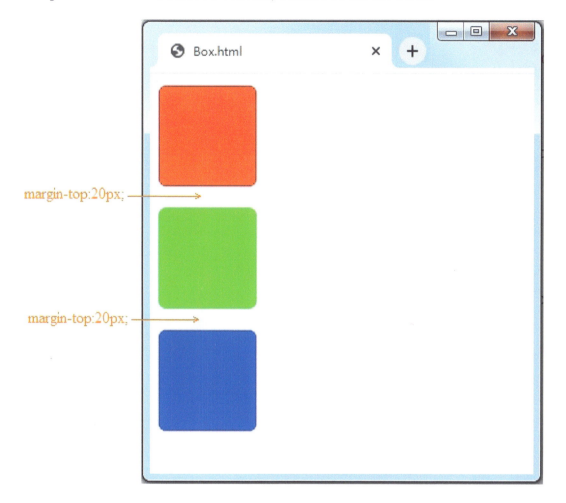

margin: CSS properties are used to create space around elements, outside of any defined borders.
(top, right, bottom, and left)
1. margin-top
2. margin -right
3. margin -bottom
4. margin -left

```
<style>
    .redBox{
        border:1px solid #cccccc;
        width:100px;
        height:100px;
        border-radius:8px;
        background-color:#ff0000;
        position:relative;
    }

    .greenBox{
        border:1px solid #cccccc;
        width:100px;
        height:100px;
        border-radius:8px;
        background-color:#00ff00;
        position:relative;
    }

    .blueBox{
        border:1px solid #cccccc;
        width:100px;
        height:100px;
        border-radius:8px;
        background-color:#0000ff;
        position:relative;
    }
</style>

<div class="redBox">

</div>
<div class="greenBox">

</div>
<div class="blueBox">

</div>
```

9. defines space around an element's content, inside of the div's box.

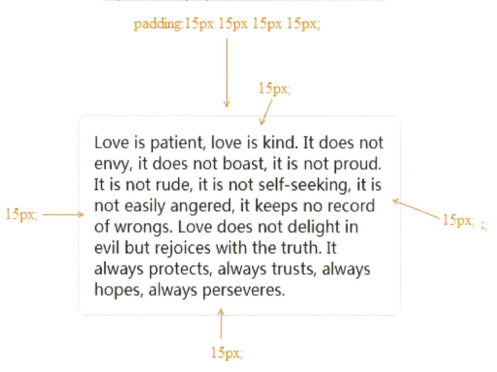

padding: CSS properties are used to generate space around an element's content, inside of any defined borders. (top, right, bottom, and left)
   1. padding-top
   2. padding-right
   3. padding-bottom
   4.padding-left

```
<style>
    .box{
        border:1px solid #cccccc;
        width:300px;
        border-radius:8px;
        padding:15px 15px 15px 15px;
    }

</style>

<div class="box">
    Love is patient, love is kind. It does not envy, it does not boast, it is not proud. It is not
rude, it is not self-seeking, it is not easily angered, it keeps no record of wrongs. Love
does not delight in evil but rejoices with the truth. It always protects, always trusts,
always hopes, always perseveres.
</div>
```

10. defines the space between two inline elements, inside of the div's box.

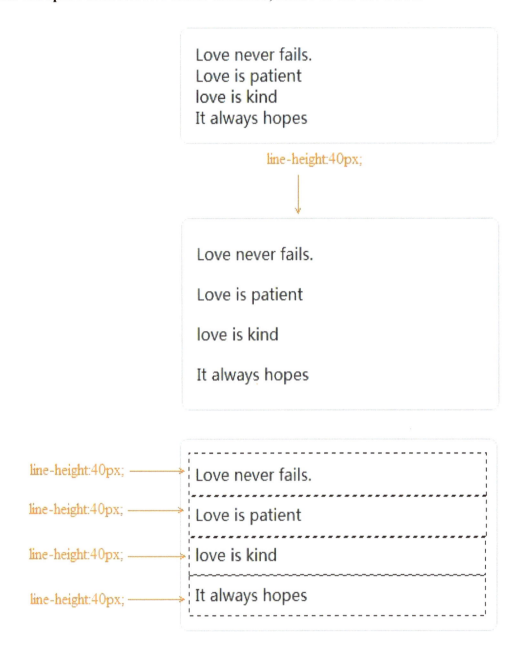

line-height: CSS property defines the space between two inline elements.
**
:** html tag break a new line.

```
<style>
  .box{
    border:1px solid #cccccc;
    width:300px;
    border-radius:8px;
    padding:15px 15px 15px 15px;
    line-height:40px;
  }

</style>

<div class="box">
  Love never fails.
  <br>
  Love is patient
  <br>
  love is kind
  <br>
  It always hopes
</div>
```

11. insert image to the div's box.

\<img\>: tag defines an image in an HTML page. src=**"shirt.jpg"** image path.

```
<style>
  .box{
    border:1px solid #cccccc;
    width:250px;
    border-radius:8px;
    padding:15px 15px 15px 15px;
  }
</style>

<div class="box">
  <img src="shirt.jpg" />
</div>
```

12. insert text below image to the div's box.

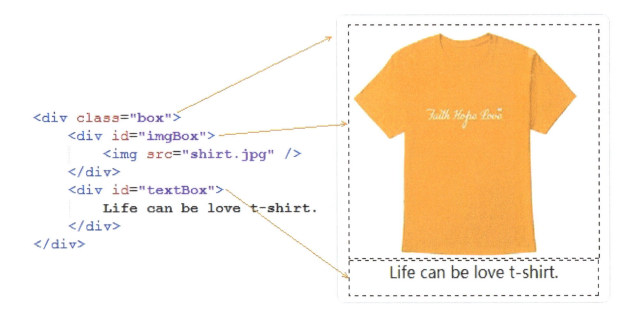

```
<div class="box">
    <div id="imgBox">
        <img src="shirt.jpg" />
    </div>
    <div id="textBox">
        Life can be love t-shirt.
    </div>
</div>
```

#id: CSS to select an element with a specific id

```html
<style>
  .box{
    border:1px solid #cccccc;
    width:250px;
    border-radius:8px;
    padding:15px 15px 15px 15px;
  }
  #imgBox{
    width:100%;
  }
  #textBox{
    text-align:center;
    width:100%;
    line-height:30px;
  }
</style>

<div class="box">
  <div id="imgBox">
    <img src="shirt.jpg" />
  </div>
  <div id="textBox">
    Life can be love t-shirt.
  </div>
</div>
```

13. Text wraps around the image.

float:left;

Love is patient, love is kind. It does not envy, it does not boast, it is not proud. It is not rude, it is not self-seeking, it is not easily angered, it keeps no record of wrongs. Love does not delight in evil but rejoices with the truth. It always protects, always trusts, always hopes, always perseveres.

Love is patient, love is kind. It does not envy, it does not boast, it is not proud. It is not rude, it is not self-seeking, it is not easily angered, it keeps no record of wrongs. Love does not delight in evil but rejoices with the truth. It always protects, always trusts, always hopes, always perseveres.

float:right;

Love is patient, love is kind. It does not envy, it does not boast, it is not proud. It is not rude, it is not self-seeking, it is not easily angered, it keeps no record of wrongs. Love does not delight in evil but rejoices with the truth. It always protects, always trusts, always hopes, always perseveres.

float: CSS property specifies how an element should float. (left, right, clear)
.box img: Descendant selector the CSS style will be used in child element.
font-family: "Times New Roman", Times, serif;

```
<style>
   .box{
      border:1px solid #cccccc;
      width:250px;
      border-radius:8px;
      padding:15px 15px 15px 15px;
      font-size:16px;
      font-family: "Times New Roman", Times, serif;
   }
   .box img{
      width:80px;
      float:left;
   }
</style>

<div class="box">
   <img src="shirt.jpg" />
Love is patient, love is kind. It does not envy, it does not boast, it is not proud. It is not
rude, it is not self-seeking, it is not easily angered, it keeps no record of wrongs. Love
does not delight in evil but rejoices with the truth. It always protects, always trusts,
always hopes, always perseveres.
</div>
```

14. unordered list: starts with the <ul> tag. Each list item starts with the <li> tag.

- Easy Learning HTML CSS
- Easy Learning Javascript
- Easy Learning Python 3

```
<style>
  #box{
    border:1px solid #cccccc;
    width:250px;
    border-radius:8px;
    padding:15px 15px 15px 15px;
    font-size:16px;
    font-family: "Times New Roman", Times, serif;
  }
</style>

<div id="box">
  <ul>
    <li>Easy Learning HTML CSS</li>
    <li>Easy Learning Javascript</li>
    <li>Easy Learning Python 3</li>
  </ul>
</div>
```

15. unordered list: insert icon image replace the black dot.

list-style-image:url('icon.jpg'); CSS property is used to specify an image that is to be used as a marker

```
<style>
  #box{
    border:1px solid #cccccc;
    width:250px;
    border-radius:8px;
    padding:15px 15px 15px 15px;
    font-size:16px;
    font-family: "Times New Roman", Times, serif;
  }

  #box ul li{
    list-style-image:url('icon.jpg');
  }
</style>

<div id="box">
  <ul>
    <li>Easy Learning HTML CSS</li>
    <li>Easy Learning Javascript</li>
    <li>Easy Learning Python 3</li>
  </ul>
</div>
```

16. Link status style

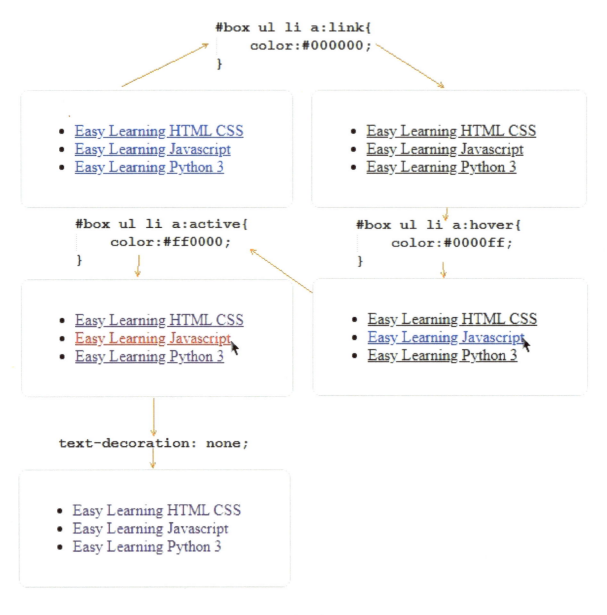

text-decoration: none; Remove text-decoration from text
li a:link: is used to select elements when not visited
li a:hover: is used to select elements when you mouse over them.
li a.active: CSS pseudo-class. It specifies <li> <a> on a state the active

```
<style>
  #box{
    border:1px solid #cccccc;
    width:250px;
    border-radius:8px;
    padding:15px 15px 15px 15px;
    font-size:16px;
    font-family: "Times New Roman", Times, serif;
  }

  #box ul li a:link{
    color:#000000;
    text-decoration: none;
  }
  #box ul li a:hover{
    color:#0000ff;
  }
  #box ul li a:active{
    color:#ff0000;
  }
</style>

<div id="box">
  <ul>
    <li><a href="#">Easy Learning HTML CSS</a></li>
    <li><a href="#">Easy Learning Javascript</a></li>
    <li><a href="#">Easy Learning Python 3</a></li>
  </ul>
</div>
```

17. Drop-down menu

list-style-type: none: CSS property Remove marker is shown in the <li>
display: block; Displays an element as a block (like <div>). It starts on a new line.
li a:hover:not(.active): is used to select elements when you mouse over them but not active

```
<style>
  ul {
    list-style-type: none;
    margin: 0;
    padding: 0;
    width: 300px;
    background-color: #eeeeee;
  }

  li a {
    display: block;
    color: #000000;
    padding: 8px 16px;
    text-decoration: none;
  }

  li a.active {
    background-color: #075272;
    color: white;
  }

  li a:hover:not(.active) {
    background-color: #59c9f9;
    color: white;
  }
</style>
```

```
<ul>
  <li><a class="active" href="#">Books</a></li>
  <li><a href="#">Easy Learning Javascript</a></li>
  <li><a href="#">Easy Learning Java</a></li>
  <li><a href="#">Easy Learning Python 3</a></li>
</ul>
```

18. Navigate menu

```
<style>
  ul {
    list-style-type: none;
    margin: 0;
    padding: 0;
    overflow: hidden;
    background-color: #333;
    position: fixed;
    top: 10;
    width: 100%;
  }

  li {
    float: left;
  }

  li a {
    display: block;
    color: white;
    text-align: center;
    padding: 15px;
    text-decoration: none;
  }

  li a:hover:not(.active) {
    background-color: #fde352;
  }

  .active {
    background-color: #fde352;
  }
</style>
<ul>
 <li><a class="active" href="#">HTML</a></li>
 <li><a href="#">CSS</a></li>
 <li><a href="#">Javascript</a></li>
 <li><a href="#">Python</a></li>
</ul>
```

19. click drop down menu

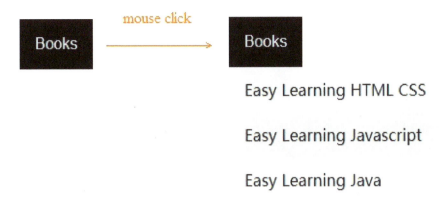

```
<style>
  .menubtn {
    background-color: #000000;
    color: white;
    padding: 16px;
    font-size: 16px;
    border: none;
    cursor: pointer;
  }

  .menudown {
    position: relative;
    display: inline-block;
    float:left;
  }

  .menudown-content {
    display: none;
    position: absolute;
    right: 0;
    background-color: #f9f9f9;
    min-width: 300px;
  }

  .menudown-content a {
    color: black;
    padding: 12px 16px;
    text-decoration: none;
    display: block;
  }
```

```css
.menudown-content a:hover {background-color: #f1f1f1}

.menudown:hover .menudown-content {
    display: block;
}

.menudown:hover .menubtn {
    background-color: #000000;
}
</style>

<div class="menudown" >
 <button class="menubtn">Books</button>
 <div class="menudown-content" style="left:0;">
  <a href="#">Easy Learning HTML CSS</a>
  <a href="#">Easy Learning Javascript</a>
  <a href="#">Easy Learning Java</a>
 </div>
</div>
```

20. login div dialog.

```
<style>
  #login{
    border:1px solid #cccccc;
    width:250px;
    border-radius:8px;
    padding:15px 15px 15px 15px;
    font-size:16px;
    font-family: "Times New Roman", Times, serif;
  }

  #login div{
    line-height:30px;
    width:100%;
  }

  .textbox{
    width:160px;
  }

  #buttonDiv{
    text-align:center;
  }

  #buttonDiv input{
    border:1px solid #cccccc;
    background-color:#ffffff;
  }
</style>
```

```html
<div id="login">
   <div>Username: <input class="textbox" type="text" id="username" /></div>
   <div>Password: <input class="textbox" type="password" id="username" /></div>
   <div id="buttonDiv">
      <input type="button" value="Login" />
      <input type="button" value="Close" />
   </div>
</div>
```

Javascript HelloWorld

Javascript is a web page dynamic interactive language that used in web development.

1. Create a helloworld.html file with Notepad and open it in your browser to see the webpage

\<html\>: tag tells the browser that this is an HTML document.
\<head\>: tag is a container for metadata about content and charset.
\<title\>: tag defines the title of the document.
\<body\>: tag defines the document's body.
\<script\>: tag is used to define a client-side script (JavaScript).
document.write(): writes HTML content to document in browser

```html
<html>
<head>
<meta http-equiv="Content-Type" content="text/html; charset=UTF-8">
<title>First Web Page</title>
</head>
  <body>
    <script type="text/javascript">
       document.write("HelloWorld");
    </script>
  </body>
</html>
```

Result:

Variable

Variable   Value

basket   =   "Apple"

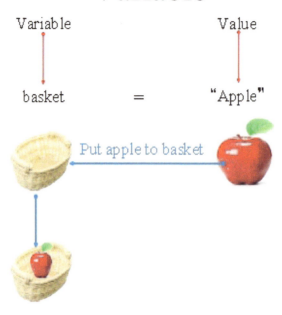

Put apple to basket

1.Create a file : Variable.html and open it in your browser

// : single comments are not executed by javascript
"": string type

```
<script type="text/javascript">
    var basket = "Apple";
    document.write(basket);
</script>
```

Result:

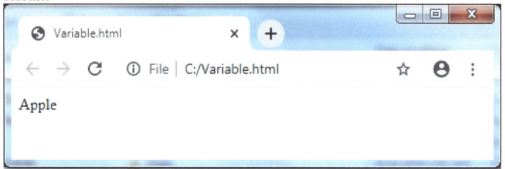

36

2.Change file : Variable.html Put "orange" **to replace** "apple".

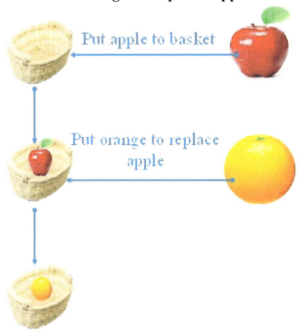

**
:** html tag wrap a new line

```
<script type="text/javascript">
    var basket = "Apple";
    document.write(basket);

    document.write("<br>");

    basket = "Orange";
    document.write(basket);
</script>
```

Run Result:

Variable and Type

Javascript is dynamic type language

1. Create a var.html file with Notepad and open it in your browser to see the webpage

typeof(): find the type of a JavaScript variable

```
<script type="text/javascript">
  var x;          //undefined
  var a=9;         //number
  var b=1.5;       //number
  var c=true;      //Boolean
  var d="abc";     //string
  var e='abc';     //string

  document.write(typeof(x) + "<br>");
  document.write(typeof(a) + "<br>");
  document.write(typeof(b) + "<br>");
  document.write(typeof(c) + "<br>");
  document.write(typeof(d) + "<br>");
  document.write(typeof(e) + "<br>");
</script>
```

Result:

undefined
number
number
boolean
string
string

Arithmetic Operator

1. Create a ArithmeticOperator.html file with Notepad and open it in your browser
Arithmetic Operator:

Add +, minus -, multiply *, divisible /, take modulo %

```
<script type="text/javascript">
    var a = 1;
    var b = 2;
    var c = 3;
    var d = 4;
    document.write(a + b); // = 3
    document.write("<br>");

    document.write(a - b); // = -1
    document.write("<br>");

    document.write(a * b); // = 2
    document.write("<br>");

    document.write(b / a); // = 2
    document.write("<br>");

    document.write(c % b); // = 1 //number remaining after divide
    document.write("<br>");
</script>
```

Function

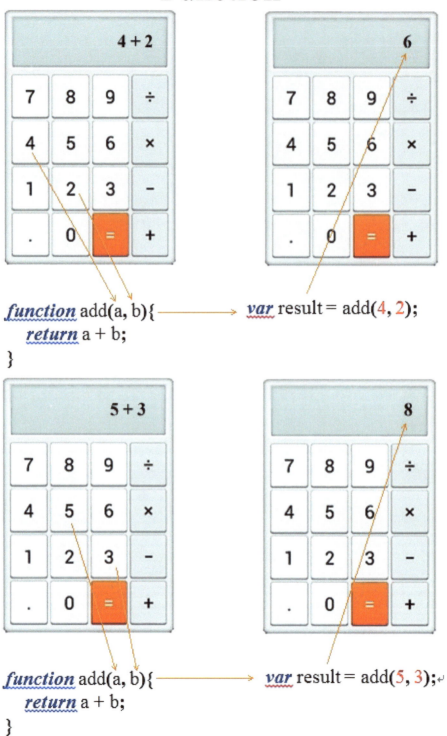

$function$ add(a, b){
   $return$ a + b;
}

var result = add(4, 2);

$function$ add(a, b){
   $return$ a + b;
}

var result = add(5, 3);↵

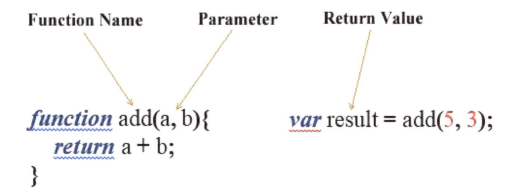

Function Name   Parameter   Return Value

$$function\ add(a,\ b)\{ \qquad\qquad var\ result = add(5,\ 3);$$
$$\quad return\ a + b;$$
$$\}$$

1.Create a file : Function.html

```
<script type="text/javascript">
  function add(a, b){
    return a + b;
  }

  var result = add(4, 2);
  document.write(result); // 6

  document.write("<br>");

  var result = add(5, 3);
  document.write(result)  // 8
</script>
```

Run Result:

6
8

2. Add 3 more functions about - , *, / to Function.html

```html
<script type="text/javascript">
  function add(a, b){
     return a + b;
  }

  function sub(a, b){
     return a - b;
  }

  function multiply(a, b){
     return a * b;
  }

  function divide(a, b){
     return a / b;
  }

  var result = add(4, 2);
  document.write(result); // 6

  document.write("<br>");

  var result = sub(4, 2);
  document.write(result)  // 2

  document.write("<br>");

  var result = multiply(4, 2);
  document.write(result)  // 8

  document.write("<br>");

  var result = divide(4, 2);
  document.write(result)  // 2

</script>
```

Class

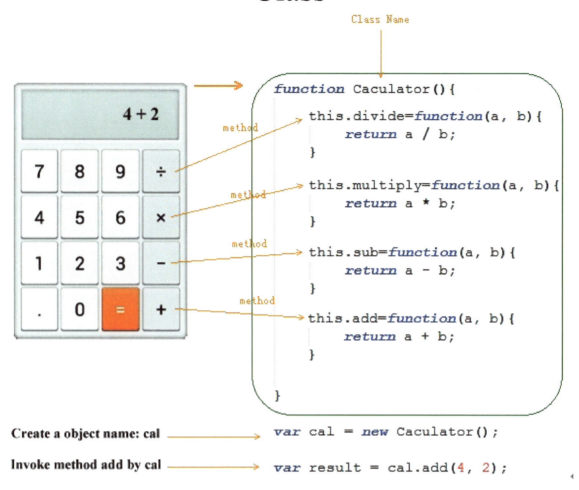

```
function Caculator(){

    this.divide=function(a, b){
        return a / b;
    }

    this.multiply=function(a, b){
        return a * b;
    }

    this.sub=function(a, b){
        return a - b;
    }

    this.add=function(a, b){
        return a + b;
    }

}
```

method

method

method

method

Create a object name: cal → `var cal = new Caculator();`

Invoke method add by cal → `var result = cal.add(4, 2);`

1.Create a file : Caculator.html

```html
<script type="text/javascript">

  function Caculator(){

    this.add=function(a, b){
      return a + b;
    }

    this.sub=function(a, b){
      return a - b;
    }

    this.multiply=function(a, b){
      return a * b;
    }

    this.divide=function(a, b){
      return a / b;
    }
  }

  var cal = new Caculator();

  var result = cal.add(4, 2);
  document.write(result); // 6

  var result = cal.sub(4, 2);
  document.write(result)  // 2

  var result = cal.multiply(4, 2);
  document.write(result)  // 8

  var result = cal.divide(4, 2);
  document.write(result)  // 2

</script>
```

Type Conversion

1. Create a TypeConversion.html

parseInt(): this is javascript default function can convert string to integer.

```
<script type="text/javascript">
    var a="1";
    var b="2";

    var result = a + b; // + concatenate two strings
    document.write(result); // = 12

    document.write("<br>");

    result = parseInt(a) + parseInt(b);
    document.write(result); // = 3
</script>
```

Result:

12
3

DOM

DOM: In Javascript every HTML element is a class object.

Document Object Model structure diagram:

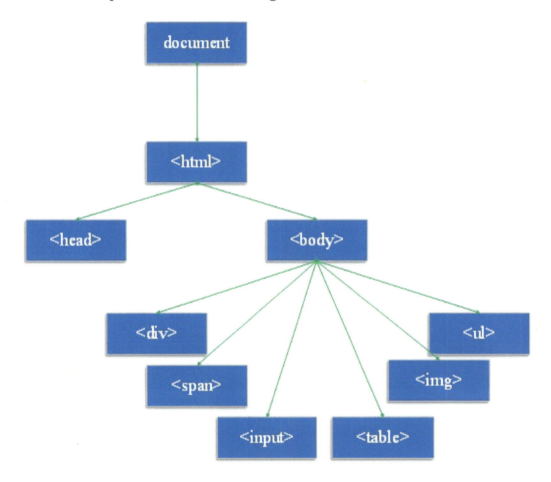

1.Create a file : getElementById.html

document.getElementById(): is a DOM method to get the element by ID attribute.
alert(): is a function to open a information window.
Obj.innerHTML: sets or returns the inner HTML content of an element.
<div>: tag defines a division or a section in an HTML document.

```html
<div id="word">Faith and Hope</div>

<script type="text/javascript">
    var divObj = document.getElementById("word");
    var htmlContent = divObj.innerHTML;
    alert(htmlContent);
</script>
```

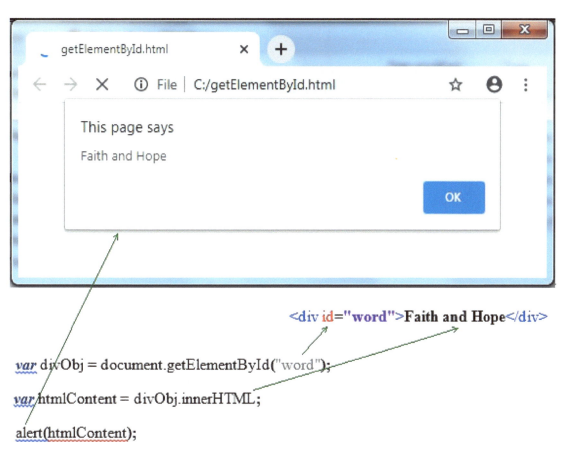

2.Change a file : getElementById.html

<input type="text" />: html tag specifies an input field where the user can enter data.

```
<input type="text" id="username" value="Joseph" />

<script type="text/javascript">
   var divObj = document.getElementById("username");
   var value = divObj.value;
   alert(value);
</script>
```

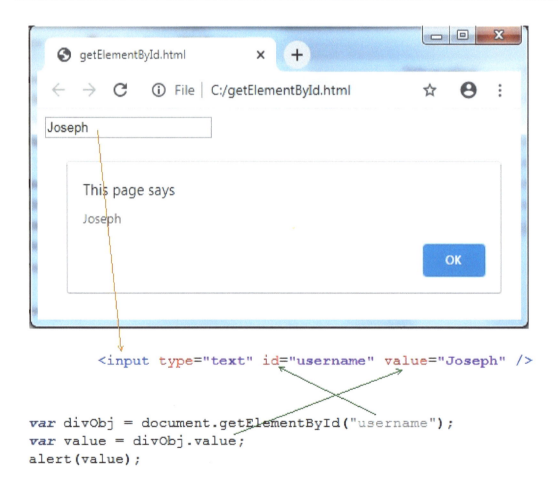

Event

1.Create a file : onClick.html

onClick: when the mouse clicks the button will call a function.
<input type="button" />: html tag defines a clickable button.

```html
<input type="text" id="username" value="Joseph" />
<input type="button" value="Click Me" onClick="doClick()" />

<script type="text/javascript">
  function doClick(){
    var divObj = document.getElementById("username");
    var value = divObj.value;
    alert(value);
  }
</script>
```

```html
<input type="text" id="username" value="Joseph" />
<input type="button" value="Click Me" onClick="doClick()" />

function doClick(){
    var divObj = document.getElementById("username");
    var value = divObj.value;
    alert(value);
}
```

Create a Web Caculator

1.Create a file : WebCaculator.html

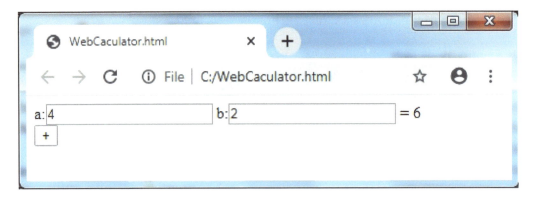

```
a:<input type="text" id="a" value="" />
b:<input type="text" id="b" value="" />
=
<span id="result"></span>
<br>
<input type="button" value="+" onClick="doAdd()" />

<script type="text/javascript">
   function doAdd(){
      var aObj = document.getElementById("a");
      var bObj = document.getElementById("b");
      var resultObj = document.getElementById("result");
      var a = parseInt(aObj.value); // Convert string to integer
      var b = parseInt(bObj.value);
      resultObj.innerHTML = a + b;
   }
</script>
```

2.Add 3 mores function - , * , / to WebCaculator.html

```html
a:<input type="text" id="a" value="" />
b:<input type="text" id="b" value="" />
=
<span id="result"></span>
<br>
<input type="button" value="+" onClick="doAdd()" />
<input type="button" value="-" onClick="doSub()" />
<input type="button" value="*" onClick="doMultiply()" />
<input type="button" value="/" onClick="doDivide()" />

<script type="text/javascript">
    function doAdd(){
        var aObj = document.getElementById("a");
        var bObj = document.getElementById("b");
        var resultObj = document.getElementById("result");
        var a = parseInt(aObj.value); // Convert string to integer
        var b = parseInt(bObj.value);
        resultObj.innerHTML = a + b;
    }

    function doSub(){
        var aObj = document.getElementById("a");
        var bObj = document.getElementById("b");
        var resultObj = document.getElementById("result");
        var a = parseInt(aObj.value); // Convert string to integer
        var b = parseInt(bObj.value);
        resultObj.innerHTML = a - b;
    }

    function doMultiply(){
        var aObj = document.getElementById("a");
        var bObj = document.getElementById("b");
        var resultObj = document.getElementById("result");
        var a = parseInt(aObj.value); // Convert string to integer
        var b = parseInt(bObj.value);
        resultObj.innerHTML = a * b;
    }
```

```
    function doDivide(){
        var aObj = document.getElementById("a");
        var bObj = document.getElementById("b");
        var resultObj = document.getElementById("result");
        var a = parseInt(aObj.value); // Convert string to integer
        var b = parseInt(bObj.value);
        resultObj.innerHTML = a / b;
    }
</script>
```

Click + button Result:

Click - button Result:

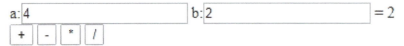

Click * button Result:

Click / button Result:

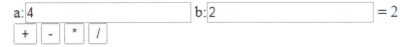

Assignment Operator

1. Create a AssignmentOperator.html file with Notepad and open it in your browser

```html
<script type="text/javascript">
   var d = 4;
   document.write(d++); // = 4 print d and then increment 1
   document.write("<br>");

   d = 4;
   document.write(++d); // = 5 increment 1 and then print d
   document.write("<br>");

   d = 4;
   document.write(d--); // = 4 print d and then decrement 1
   document.write("<br>");

   d = 4;
   document.write(--d); // = 3 decrement 1 and then print d

   var result = 10;
   result = result + 1;
   document.write(result); // = 11
   document.write("<br>");

   result = 10;
   result++;
   document.write(result); // = 11
   document.write("<br>");

   result = 10;
   result += 1;
   document.write(result);  // = 11
   document.write("<br>");
</script>
```

2. Create a quantity adder and subtracter quantity.html

Click + button to increase the quantity by 1, and click - button to decrease the quantity by 1.

Quantity:

```html
<br>
<input type="text" style="width:30px" id="quantity" value="1" />
<input type="button" value="+" onClick="doAdd()" />
<input type="button" value="-" onClick="doSub()" />

<script type="text/javascript">
  function doAdd(){
     var quantityObj = document.getElementById("quantity");
     var value = parseInt(quantityObj.value);
     value++
     quantityObj.value = value;
  }

  function doSub(){
     var quantityObj = document.getElementById("quantity");
     var value = parseInt(quantityObj.value);
     value--
     quantityObj.value = value;
  }
</script>
```

Relational Operator

1. Create a RelationalOperator.html file with Notepad and open it in your browser

Relational operators only two value: true, false

```
<script type="text/javascript">

    document.write(1 > 2); // false
    document.write("<br>");

    document.write(1 >= 1); // true
    document.write("<br>");

    document.write(1 < 2); // true
    document.write("<br>");

    document.write(1 <= 2); // true
    document.write("<br>");

    document.write(1 == 1); // true
    document.write("<br>");

    document.write(1 != 2); // true

</script>
```

If Conditional Statement

If statement
1. if(expression){statement}
2. if (expression) { statement } else { statement }
3. if (expression) {statement } else if { statement }

1. Create a If.html file with Notepad and open it in your browser

Score example:
if score == 5 : Excellent
else if score == 4:   Good
else: Need to catch up

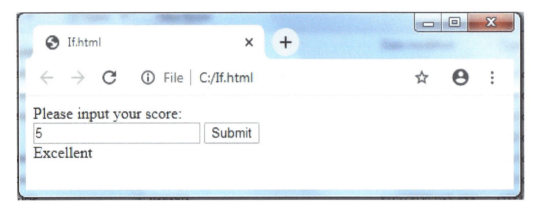

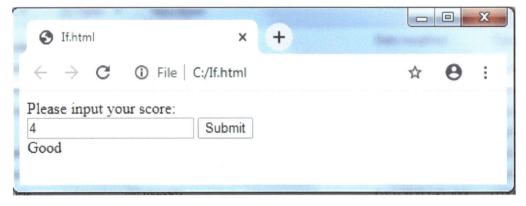

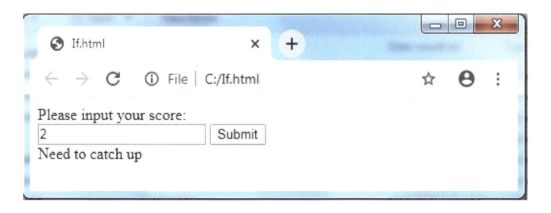

Please input your score:
```html
<br>
<input type="text"  id="score" value="" />
<input type="button" value="Submit" onClick="doSubmit()" />
<br>
<span id="message"></span>

<script type="text/javascript">
   function doSubmit(){
      var scoreObj = document.getElementById("score");
      var messageObj = document.getElementById("message");

      var score = parseInt(scoreObj.value);
      if (score == 5) {
         messageObj.innerHTML = "Excellent";
      } else if (score == 4) {
         messageObj.innerHTML = "Good";
      } else {
         messageObj.innerHTML = "Need to catch up";
      }
   }
</script>
```

Logic Operator

1. Create a LogicOperator.html file with Notepad and open it in your browser

Logical Operator: and &&, or ||, not !
   1. && returns true if both sides of the operation are true, otherwise false
   2. || The result is false when both sides of the operation are false, otherwise true;
   3. ! if returns true, the result is false, otherwise is true

```html
<script type="text/javascript">
   document.write(true && false); // false
   document.write("<br>");

   document.write(false && true); // false
   document.write("<br>");

   document.write(false && false); // false
   document.write("<br>");

   document.write(true && true); // true
   document.write("<br>");

   document.write(true || false); // true
   document.write("<br>");

   document.write(false || true); // true
   document.write("<br>");

   document.write(true || true); // true
   document.write("<br>");

   document.write(false || false); // false
   document.write("<br>");

   document.write(!true); // false
   document.write("<br>");

   document.write(!false); // true
   document.write("<br>");
</script>
```

2. Create a LogicOperator2.html

```html
<script type="text/javascript">

    document.write(1>2 && 3>4) // = false
    document.write(2>1 && 3>4) // = false

    document.write("-------------")

    document.write(2>1 || 3>4) // = true
    document.write(2>1 || 3>4) // = true
    document.write(1>2 || 3>4) // = false

</script>
```

3. Payroll tax example:

Tax amount = salary * tax rate
level:
500 -- 2000 $: tax rate 10%
2000--5000 $:   tax rate 15%
5000-- 20000 $: tax rate 20%
    More than 20000$:   tax rate 30%

```javascript
<script type="text/javascript">
  var salary = 10000;
  var tax = 0;
  if (salary >= 500 && salary < 2000) {
    tax = salary * 0.1;
  } else if (salary >= 2000 && salary < 5000) {
    tax = salary * 0.15;
  } else if (salary >= 5000 && salary < 20000) {
    tax = salary * 0.2;
  } else {
    tax = salary * 0.3;
  }
  document.write("tax amount=" + tax);
</script>
```

Result:

tax amount=2000

2. Create a WebTax.html

Input salary and then click Calculate Tax button

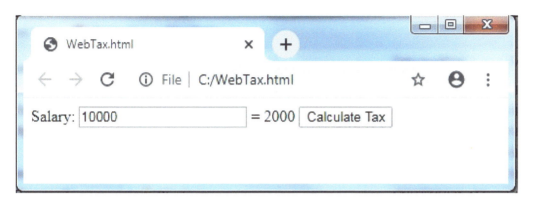

```
Salary: <input type="text" id="salary" value="" />
=
<span id="tax"></span>
<input type="button" value="Calculate Tax" onClick="doTax()" />

<script type="text/javascript">

  function doTax(){
    var salaryObj = document.getElementById("salary");
    var salary = parseInt(salaryObj.value);
    var tax = 0;
    if (salary >= 500 && salary < 2000) {
      tax = salary * 0.1;
    } else if (salary >= 2000 && salary < 5000) {
      tax = salary * 0.15;
    } else if (salary >= 5000 && salary < 20000) {
      tax = salary * 0.2;
    } else {
      tax = salary * 0.3;
    }
    document.getElementById("tax").innerHTML = tax;
  }

</script>
```

Switch Statement

1. Create a switch.html file with Notepad and open it in your browser

Input a number 1 , 2, 3
   1 : Pay by Visa Card
   2 : Pay by Master Card
   3: Pay by Paypal
      Otherwise Pay by face to face

```
<script type="text/javascript">

  var num = 1;

  switch (num) {
    case 1:
        document.write("Pay by Visa Card");
        break; // terminate the code to continue execution
    case 2:
        document.write("Pay by Master Card");
        break;
    case 3:
        document.write("Pay by Paypal");
        break;
    default:
        document.write("Pay by face to face");
  }

</script>
```

Result:

Pay by Visa Card

2. Create a WebPay.html

this: current element object

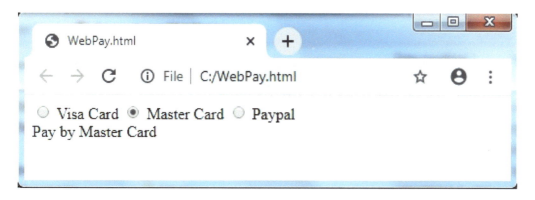

```
<input type="radio" name="card" value="1" onclick="doPay(this)" /> Visa Card
<input type="radio" name="card" value="2" onclick="doPay(this)" /> Master Card
<input type="radio" name="card" value="3" onclick="doPay(this)" /> Paypal
<br>
<span id="result"></span>

<script type="text/javascript">

   function doPay(obj){
      var num = parseInt(obj.value);
      var resultObj = document.getElementById("result");

      switch (num) {
        case 1:
           resultObj.innerHTML = "Pay by Visa Card";
           break;
        case 2:
           resultObj.innerHTML = "Pay by Master Card";
           break;
        case 3:
           resultObj.innerHTML = "Pay by Paypal";
           break;
        default:
           resultObj.innerHTML = "Pay by face to face";
      }
   }
</script>
```

While Loop Statement

```
while(expression){
    statement;
}
```
continues execution if the expression is true, otherwise exits loop

```
var i = 0;
while (i < 10)          i=0 < 10 true executes the loop code
{
    document.write(i+".");      i=1
    i++;
}


while (i < 10)          i=1 < 10 true executes the loop code
{
    document.write(i+".");      i=2
    i++;
}


while (i < 10)          i=2 < 10 true executes the loop code
{
    document.write(i+".");
    i++;                        i=3
}

        Until i = 9
while (i < 10)          i=9 < 10 true executes the loop code
{
    document.write(i+".");      i=10
    i++;
}


while (i < 10)              i=10 < 10 False terminated
{
    document.write(i+".");      i=11
    i++;
}

    While Loop is terminated
```

1. Create a WhileLoop.html file with Notepad and open it in your browser

```
<script type="text/javascript">

    var i = 0;
    while (i < 10)
    {
        document.write(i+",");
        i++;
    }

</script>
```

Result:

0,1,2,3,4,5,6,7,8,9,

For Loop Statement

```
for (var i = 0; i < 10; i++) {
    document.write(i + ",");
}
```
i=0 < 10 true executes the loop code

i++

```
for (var i = 0; i < 10; i++) {
    document.write(i + ",");
}
```
i=1 < 10 true executes the loop code

i++

```
for (var i = 0; i < 10; i++) {
    document.write(i + ",");
}
```
i=2 < 10 true executes the loop code

i++

Until i = 9

```
for (var i = 0; i < 10; i++) {
    document.write(i + ",");
}
```
i=9 < 10 true executes the loop code

i++

```
for (var i = 0; i < 10; i++) {
    document.write(i + ",");
}
```
i=10 < 10 False terminated

i++

For Loop is terminated

1. Create a ForLoop.html file with Notepad and open it in your browser

```
<script type="text/javascript">

  for (var i = 0; i < 10; i++) {
     document.write(i + ",");
  }

</script>
```

Result:

0,1,2,3,4,5,6,7,8,9,

One-Dimensional Array

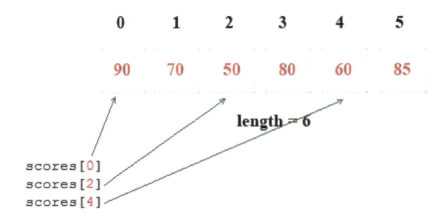

1. Create a OneArray.html file with Notepad and open it in your browser

```
<script type="text/javascript">

   // One-dimensional array definition and initialization
   var scores = [ 90, 70, 50, 80, 60, 85 ];

   document.write(scores[0] + "<br>");
   document.write(scores[2] + "<br>");
   document.write(scores[4] + "<br>");

</script>
```

Result:

90
50
60

2. Change OneArray.html print all scores of the array

Scores.length: the total count of array

```html
<script type="text/javascript">

  var scores = [ 90, 70, 50, 80, 60, 85 ];

  //print all the scores of the array
  for (var i = 0; i < scores.length; i++) {
     document.write(scores[i] + ",");
  }

</script>
```

Result:

90,70,50,80,60,85,

3. Change OneArray.html print all scores of the array

```html
<script type="text/javascript">

    // Dynamically define a one-dimensional array
    var scores = new Array();
    scores[0] = 90;
    scores[1] = 70;
    scores[2] = 50;
    scores[3] = 80;
    scores[4] = 60;
    scores[5] = 85;

    //print all the scores of the array
    for (var i = 0; i < scores.length; i++) {
        document.write(scores[i] + ",");
    }

</script>
```

Result:

90,70,50,80,60,85,

Select All Check Box

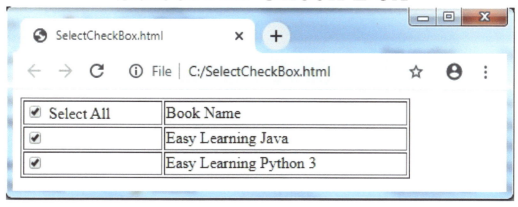

**1. Create a SelectCheckBox.html file with Notepad and open it in your browser
document.getElementsByName():** get an array of elements with the same name
checked: if the checkbox is checked

```html
<table width="400" border="1">
  <tr>
    <td><input type="checkbox" onclick="checkAll(this)" /> Select All</td>
    <td>Book Name</td>
  </tr>
  <tr>
    <td><input type="checkbox" name="book" /></td>
    <td>Easy Learning Java</td>
  </tr>
  <tr>
    <td><input type="checkbox" name="book" /></td>
    <td>Easy Learning Python 3</td>
  </tr>
</table>
<script language="JavaScript">
  function checkAll(obj)
  {
    var bookArray=document.getElementsByName("book");
    for(var i=0;i<bookArray.length;i++)
    {
      bookArray[i].checked=obj.checked;
    }
  }
</script>
```

Two-Dimensional Array

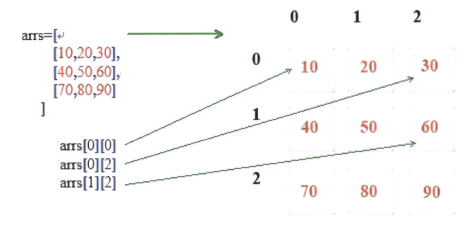

1. Create a TwoArray.html file with Notepad and open it in your browser

```
<script type="text/javascript">

    // Two-dimensional array definition and initialization
    var arrs =[
      [ 10, 20, 30 ],
      [ 40, 50, 60 ],
      [ 70, 80, 90 ]
    ];

    document.write(arrs[0][0] + "<br>");
    document.write(arrs[0][2] + "<br>");
    document.write(arrs[1][2] + "<br>");

</script>
```

Result:

10
30
60

2. Create a TwoArray2.html file with Notepad and open it in your browser

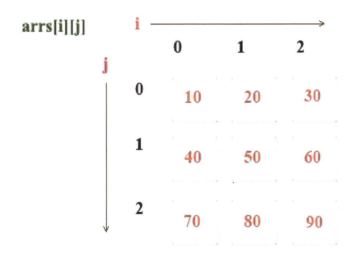

```
<script type="text/javascript">

    var arrs =[
       [ 10, 20, 30 ],
       [ 40, 50, 60 ],
       [ 70, 80, 90 ]
    ];

    // i: row index, j: column index
    for (var i = 0; i < arrs.length; i++) {
       for (var j = 0; j < arrs[i].length; j++) {
          document.write(arrs[i][j]);
          document.write(" ");
       }
       document.write("<br>");
    }

</script>
```

Find Dog Game

1. Draw buttons according to two-dimensional array maps

```
var maps =[
    [ 1, 1, 1, 1 ],
    [ 1, 1, 1, 1 ],
    [ 1, 2, 1, 1 ],
    [ 1, 1, 1, 1 ]
];
```

```html
<style>
  input{
    width:40px;
    height:40px;
  }
</style>

<span id="result"></span>

<script type="text/javascript">
  var maps =[
    [ 1, 1, 1, 1 ],
    [ 1, 1, 1, 1 ],
    [ 1, 2, 1, 1 ],
    [ 1, 1, 1, 1 ]
  ];
  var mapHTML = "";
  for (var i = 0; i < maps.length; i++) {
    for (var j = 0; j < maps[i].length; j++) {
      mapHTML +="<input type='button' value=' ' />";
    }
    mapHTML +="<br>";
  }
  document.getElementById("result").innerHTML = mapHTML;
</script>
```

2. Fill in the value of the array into the button, and add a button click event, if button value is 1 becomes *, if button value is 2 becomes Dog

```
            1:  *↵
            2:  Dog↵

var maps =[
    [ 1, 1, 1, 1 ],        ──────→
    [ 1, 1, 1, 1 ],
    [ 1, 2, 1, 1 ],
    [ 1, 1, 1, 1 ]
];
```

1: *
2: Dog

```html
<style>
  input{
    width:40px;
    height:40px;
  }
</style>

<span id="result"></span>

<script type="text/javascript">
  var maps =[
    [ 1, 1, 1, 1 ],
    [ 1, 1, 1, 1 ],
    [ 1, 2, 1, 1 ],
    [ 1, 1, 1, 1 ]
  ];

  var mapHTML = "";
  for (var i = 0; i < maps.length; i++) {
    for (var j = 0; j < maps[i].length; j++) {
      mapHTML +="<input type='button' value=' '
onClick='doButtonClick(this,"+maps[i][j]+")' />";
    }
    mapHTML +="<br>";
  }
  document.getElementById("result").innerHTML = mapHTML;
```

```
    function doButtonClick(obj,value){
        if(value == 1){
            obj.value = "*";
        }else if(value == 2){
            obj.value = "Dog";
        }
    }
</script>
```

3. Print random numbers 0-9

Math.random(): returns a random number between 0 and 1.
Math.floor(): rounds a number downwards to the nearest integer

```
<script type="text/javascript">
    for(var i=0;i<10;i++){
        var num = Math.floor(Math.random() * 10)
        document.write(num + ", ");
    }
</script>
```

Result:

9, 3, 9, 0, 4, 1, 0, 3, 4, 5,

4. Randomly generate 1- 2 initialize two-dimensional array, Fill in the value of the array into the button, and add a button click event, if button value is 1 becomes *, if button value is 2 becomes Dog

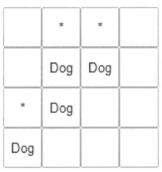

1:   *
2:   Dog

```
<style>
  input{
    width:40px;
    height:40px;
  }
</style>

<span id="result"></span>

<script type="text/javascript">
  var maps =[
    [ 0, 0, 0, 0 ],
    [ 0, 0, 0, 0 ],
    [ 0, 0, 0, 0 ],
    [ 0, 0, 0, 0 ]
  ];

  for (var i = 0; i < maps.length; i++) {
    for (var j = 0; j < maps[i].length; j++) {
      var num = Math.floor(Math.random()*2)+1
      maps[i][j] = num;
    }
  }
```

```javascript
    var mapHTML = "";
    for (var i = 0; i < maps.length; i++) {
        for (var j = 0; j < maps[i].length; j++) {
            mapHTML +="<input type='button' value=' '
onClick='doButtonClick(this,"+maps[i][j]+")' />";
        }
        mapHTML +="<br>";
    }
    document.getElementById("result").innerHTML = mapHTML;


    function doButtonClick(obj,value){
        if(value == 1){
            obj.value = "*";
        }else if(value == 2){
            obj.value = "Dog";
        }
    }
}
</script>
```

Secondary Linkage Drop-down

1. Create a Drop-down.html file with Notepad and open it in your browser

window.onload: execute a function after a page has been loaded
document.createElement(): create a html element

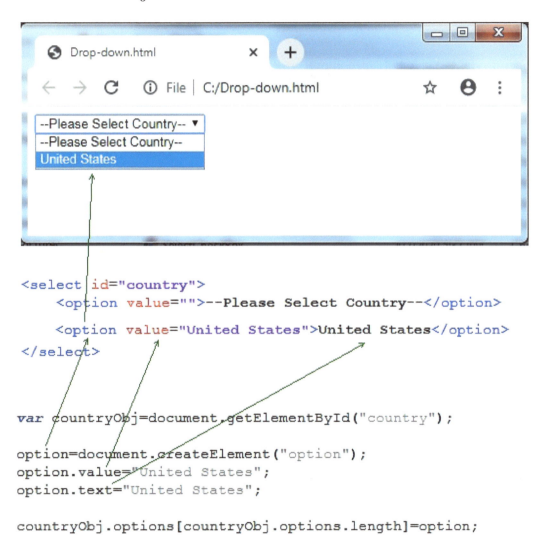

```
<select id="country">
    <option value="">--Please Select Country--</option>

    <option value="United States">United States</option>
</select>


var countryObj=document.getElementById("country");

option=document.createElement("option");
option.value="United States";
option.text="United States";

countryObj.options[countryObj.options.length]=option;
```

```html
<select id="country">
  <option value="">--Please Select Country--</option>
</select>

<script type="text/javascript">

  window.onload=function()
  {
    var countryObj=document.getElementById("country");

    option=document.createElement("option");
    option.text="United States";
    option.value="United States";

    countryObj.options[countryObj.options.length]=option;
  }

</script>
```

2. Add more options by countryArray

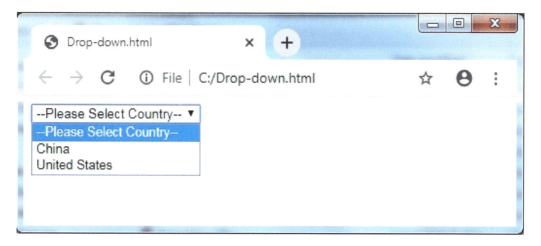

```
<select id="country">
   <option value="">--Please Select Country--</option>
</select>

<script type="text/javascript">

   var countryArray=["China", "United States"];

   window.onload=function()
   {
     var countryObj=document.getElementById("country");

     for(var i=0;i<countryArray.length;i++)
      {
        var option=document.createElement("option");
        option.text=countryArray[i];
        option.value=countryArray[i];
        countryObj.options[countryObj.options.length]=option;
      }
   }

</script>
```

3. Add province options

selectedIndex: sets or returns the index of the selected option in a drop-down list.

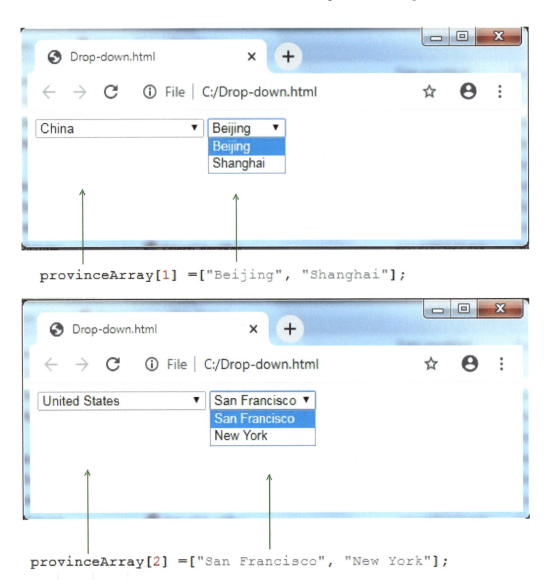

```
provinceArray[1] =["Beijing", "Shanghai"];
```

```
provinceArray[2] =["San Francisco", "New York"];
```

```html
<select id="country" onchange="doCountryChange(this)" >
   <option value="">--Please Select Country--</option>
</select>

<select id="province" >
</select>

<script type="text/javascript">
   var countryArray=["China", "United States"];

   var provinceArray = new Array();
    provinceArray[0] =[];
    provinceArray[1] =["Beijing", "Shanghai"];
    provinceArray[2] =["San Francisco", "New York"];

   window.onload=function()
   {
      var country=document.getElementById("country");
      for(var i=0;i<countryArray.length;i++)
      {
         var option=document.createElement("option");
         option.text=countryArray[i];
         option.value=countryArray[i];
         country.options[country.options.length]=option;
      }
   }

   function doCountryChange(obj)
   {
      var provinceObj=document.getElementById("province");
      provinceObj.options.length=0; // clear all
      var index=obj.selectedIndex;
      for(var i=0;i<provinceArray[index].length;i++)
      {
         var option=document.createElement("option");
         option.text=provinceArray[index][i];
         option.value=provinceArray[index][i];
         provinceObj.options[provinceObj.options.length]=option;
      }
   }
</script>
```

Event

Event List:

Onblur	element loses focus
Onchange	changes the contents
Onclick	mouse click on an object
Ondblclick	mouse double click on an object
Onerror	An error occurred while loading a document or image
Onfocus	element gets focus
Onkeydown	The key of a keyboard is pressed
Onkeypress	The key of a keyboard is pressed
Onkeyup	The key of a keyboard is released
Onload	a page or image is loaded
Onmousedown	a mouse button is pressed
Onmousemove	mouse is moved
Onmouseout	mouse is moved out from an element
Onmouseover	mouse is moved over an element
Onmouseup	mouse button is released
Onreset	reset button is clicked
Onresize	window or frame is resized
Onselect	text is selected
Onsubmit	submit button is clicked
Onunload	exit page

Login Web Page

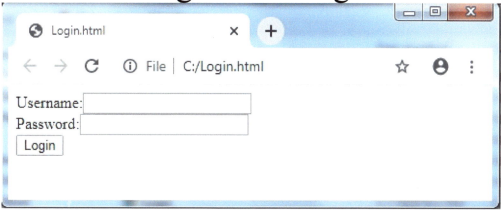

1. Create a Login.html file with Notepad and open it in your browser

```html
Username:<input type="text" id="username"  value="" /> <br>
Password:<input type="password"  id="pwd"  value="" /> <br>
<input type="button" value="Login" onclick="checkLogin()" />

<script  type="text/javascript">
  function checkLogin()
  {
     var usernameObj=document.getElementById("username");
     var pwdObj=document.getElementById("pwd");

     if(usernameObj.value=="")
     {
       alert("Please input username !");
       return;
     }

     if(pwdObj.value=="")
     {
       alert("Please input password !");
       return;
     }

     alert("login successfull !");
  }
</script>
```

2. Create a Login.html file with Notepad and open it in your browser

document.onkeypress: the event occurs when the user presses a key.

```html
Username:<input type="text" id="username" value="" />
<br>
Password:<input type="password" id="pwd" value="" />
<br>
<input type="button" value="Login" onclick="checkLogin()" />

<script type="text/javascript">
   document.onkeypress=function(event)
   {
      var ext=window.event?window.event:event;
      var key=ext.keyCode?ext.keyCode:ext.which;
      if(key==13) // press enter key will be invoked
      {
         checkLogin();
      }
   }

   function checkLogin()
   {
      var usernameObj=document.getElementById("username");
      var pwdObj=document.getElementById("pwd");

      if(usernameObj.value=="")
      {
         alert("Please input username !");
         return;
      }

      if(pwdObj.value=="")
      {
         alert("Please input password !");
         return;
      }

      alert("login successfull !");
   }
</script>
```

MouseOver Thumbnail to Larger

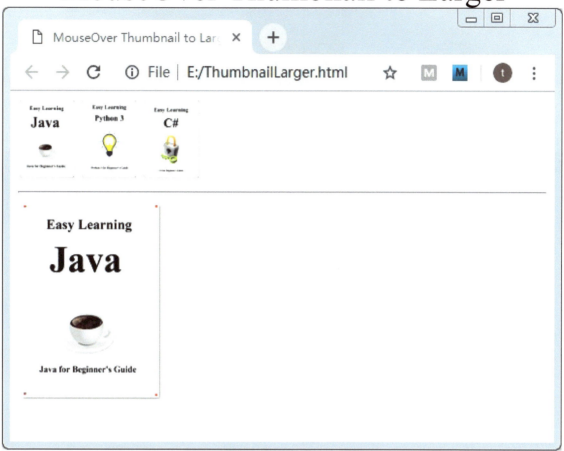

1. Create a ThumbnailLarger.html **file with** Notepad **and open it in your browser**

\<img\>: tag defines an image in an HTML page.

```
<img src="images/java.jpg" width="60" onmouseover="zoomImage(this)" />
<img src="images/python.jpg" width="60" onmouseover="zoomImage(this)" />
<img src="images/csharp.jpg" width="60" onmouseover="zoomImage(this)" />
<hr>
<img id="image" src="" />
<script type="text/javascript">
  function zoomImage(obj)
  {
     document.getElementById("image").src = obj.src;
  }
</script>
```

Element Hierarchy

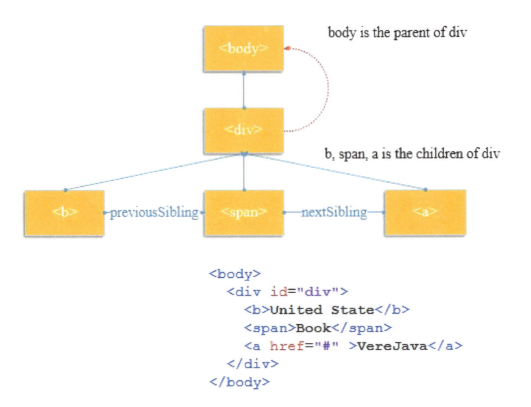

body is the parent of div

b, span, a is the children of div

previousSibling   nextSibling

```html
<body>
  <div id="div">
    <b>United State</b>
    <span>Book</span>
    <a href="#" >VereJava</a>
  </div>
</body>
```

1. Change ElementHierarchy.html to get all child nodes.

obj.childNodes: get all child nodes of current node
obj. nodeName: get the node's name
obj. nodeType: get the node's type
obj. innerHTML: get the node's html content

<b>: tag specifies bold text.
<a>: tag defines a hyperlink, which is used to link from one page to another.

```html
<body>
 <div id="div">
  <b>United State</b>
  <span>Book</span>
  <a href="#" >VereJava</a>
 </div>
 <hr>
 <input type="button" value="Get Parent Node" onclick="doGetParentNode()" />
</body>

<script type="text/javascript">
  function doGetParentNode()
  {
    var divObj=document.getElementById("div");
    alert(divObj.parentNode.nodeName);
  }
</script>
```

2. Change ElementHierarchy.html get all child nodes

obj.childNodes: get all child nodes of current node
obj.nodeName: get the parent node's name
obj.nodeType: get the parent node's type
obj.innerHTML: get the parent node's html content

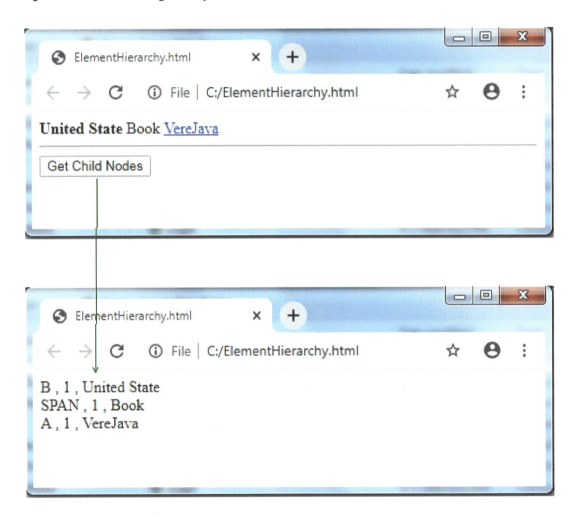

```html
<body>
 <div id="div">
   <b>United State</b>
   <span>Book</span>
   <a href="#" >VereJava</a>
 </div>
 <hr>
 <input type="button" value="Get Child Nodes" onclick="doGetChildNodes()" />
</body>

<script type="text/javascript">

  function doGetChildNodes()
  {
     var div=document.getElementById("div");
     var childNodes=div.childNodes;
     for(var i=0;i<childNodes.length;i++)
     {
       if(childNodes[i].nodeType==1)
       {
         document.write(childNodes[i].nodeName+" , ");
         document.write(childNodes[i].nodeType+" , ");
         document.write(childNodes[i].innerHTML+"<br>");
       }
     }
  }
</script>
```

3. Change ElementHierarchy.html get book node's previous and next node

obj. previousSibling: get previous node of current node
obj. nextSibling: get next node of current node

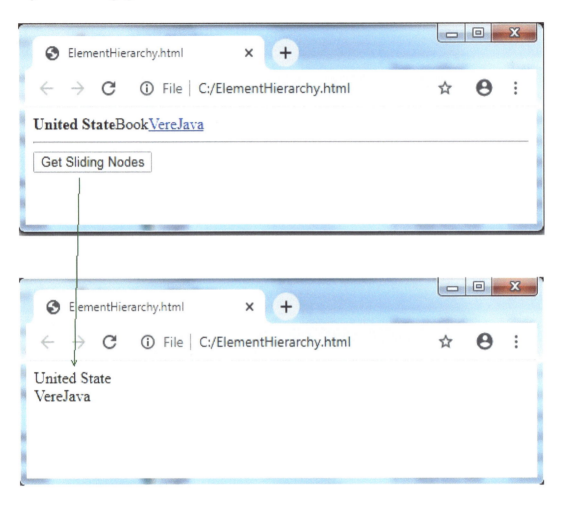

```html
<body>
 <div id="div">
   <b>United State</b><span id="book">Book</span><a href="#" >VereJava</a>
 </div>
 <hr>
 <input type="button" value="Get Sliding Nodes" onclick="doGetSliding()" />
</body>

<script type="text/javascript">

  function doGetSliding()
  {
    var bookObj=document.getElementById("book");
    document.write(bookObj.previousSibling.innerHTML+"<br>");
    document.write(bookObj.nextSibling.innerHTML);
  }

</script>
```

Create Text Node

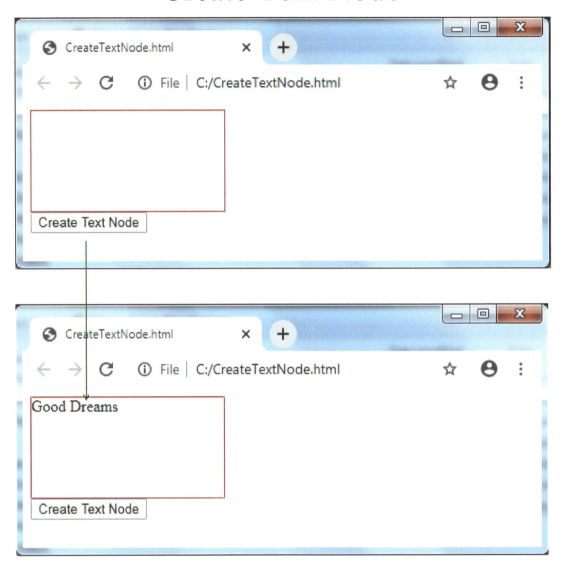

1. Create a CreateTextNode.html file with Notepad and open it in your browser

obj. createTextNode: creates a Text Node with the specified text
obj. appendChild: appends a node as the last child of a node

```html
<style>
   div{
      width:200px;
      height:100px;
      border:1px solid #ff0000;
   }
</style>

<div id="div"></div>
<input type="button" value="Create Text Node" onclick="doCreateTextNode()" />

<script type="text/javascript">

   function doCreateTextNode()
   {
      var divObj = document.getElementById("div");
      var newNode=document.createTextNode("Good Dreams");
      divObj.appendChild(newNode);
   }

</script>
```

2. Create a CreateElement.html file with Notepad and open it in your browser

obj. createElement: creates an Element Node with the specified name
obj. appendChild: appends a node as the last child of a node

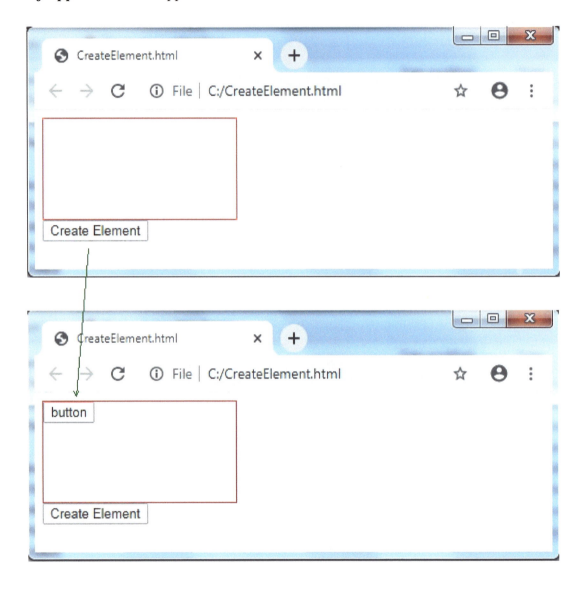

```
<style>
   div{
      width:200px;
      height:100px;
      border:1px solid #ff0000;
   }
</style>

<div id="div">
</div>

<input type="button" value="Create Element" onclick="doCreateElement()" />

<script type="text/javascript">

   function doCreateElement()
   {
      var divObj = document.getElementById("div");
      var buttonElement=document.createElement("input");
      buttonElement.type="button";
      buttonElement.value="button";
      divObj.appendChild(buttonElement);
   }

</script>
```

Delete Node

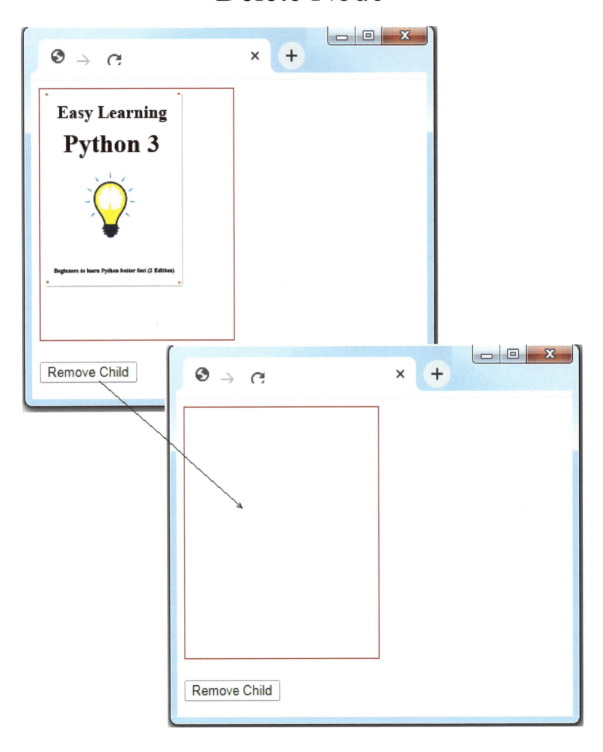

1. Create a DeleteNode.html file with Notepad and open it in your browser

obj. removeChild: removes a specified child node

```
<style>
  div{
    width:200px;
    height:250px;
    border:1px solid #ff0000;
  }
</style>

<div id="div1">
  <img id="image" src="python.jpg" />
</div>
<br>
<input type="button" value="Remove Child" onclick="doRemoveChild()" />

<script type="text/javascript">

  function doRemoveChild()
  {
    var div=document.getElementById("div1");
    var img=document.getElementById("image");
    div.removeChild(img);
  }

</script>
```

Replace Node

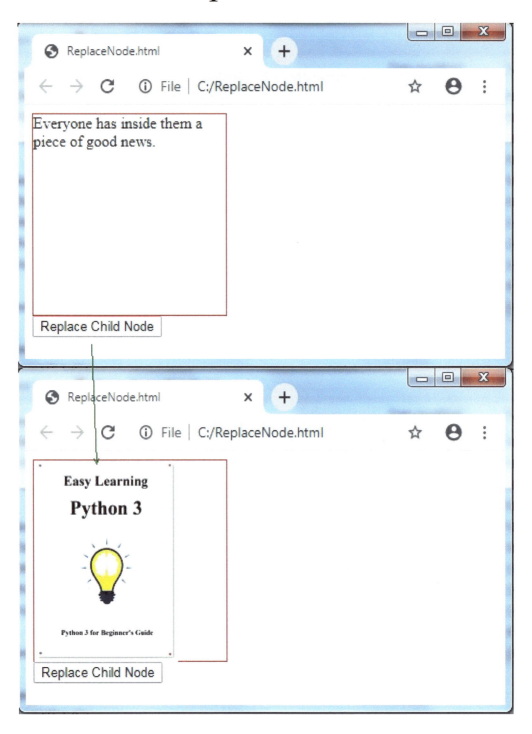

1. Create a ReplaceNode.html file with Notepad and open it in your browser

obj. replaceChild: replaces a child node with a new node

```html
<style>
  #div1{
    width:200px;
    height:200px;
    border:1px solid #ff0000;
  }
</style>

<div id="div1">Everyone has inside them a piece of good news.</div>
<input type="button" value="Replace Child Node" onclick="doReplaceChild()" />

<script type="text/javascript">

  function doReplaceChild()
  {
    var imgNode=document.createElement("img");
    imgNode.src="python.jpg";
    var div1=document.getElementById("div1");
    div1.replaceChild(imgNode,div1.childNodes[0]);
  }

</script>
```

Add Contact Example

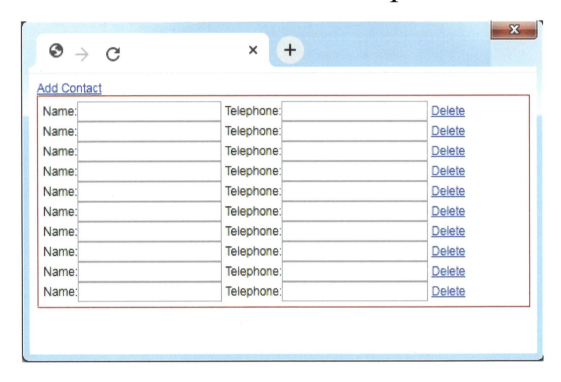

1. Create a AddContactExample.html file with Notepad and open it in your browser

```html
<style>
  #div{
    border:1px solid #ff0000;
    width:550px;
  }
</style>

<a href="javascript:void(0)" onclick="addContact()" >Add Contact</a>
<div id="div">
  <div id="contact">
    Name:<input type="text" name="user" />
    Telephone:<input type="text" name="telephone" />
    <a href="javascript:void(0)" onclick="deleteNode(this)" >Delete</a>
  </div>
</div>

<script type="text/javascript">

  function addContact()
  {
    var contact=document.getElementById("contact");
    var newNone=contact.cloneNode(true);

    var div=document.getElementById("div");
    div.appendChild(newNone);
  }

  function deleteNode(obj)
  {
    if(obj.parentNode.parentNode.childNodes.length>1)
      obj.parentNode.removeNode(true);
  }

</script>
```

CSS Style Font

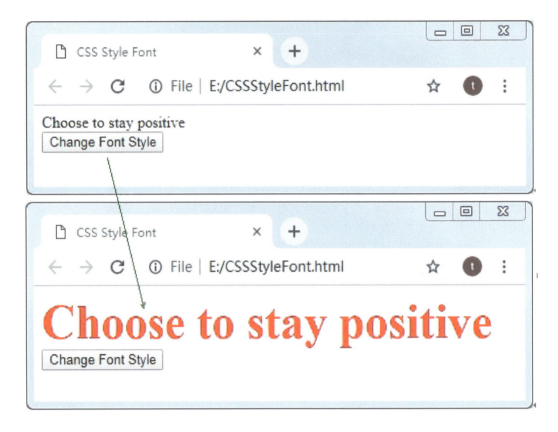

1. Create a CSSStyleFont.html file with Notepad and open it in your browser

```
<div id="div">Choose to stay positive</div>
<input type="button" value="Change Font Style" onclick="doChangeFont()" />

<script type="text/javascript">
  function doChangeFont()
  {
    var div=document.getElementById("div");
    div.style.fontSize=48+"px";
    div.style.fontWeight="bold";
    div.style.color="#ff0000";
  }
</script>
```

CSS Change Class Selector

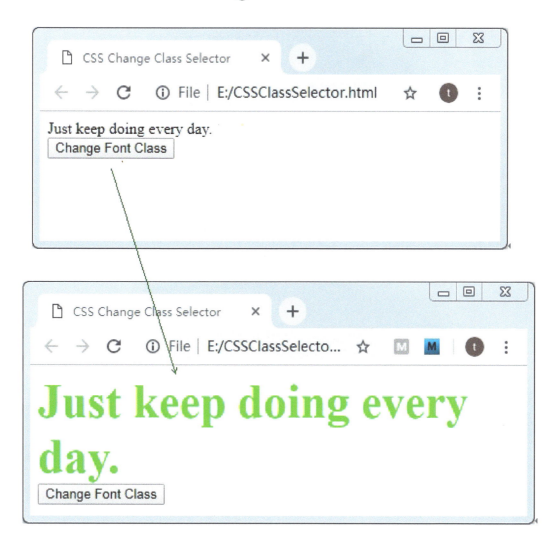

1. Create a CSSClassSelector.html file with Notepad and open it in your browser

```
<style type="text/css">
  .smallFont{
     font-size:12px;
     color:#ff0000;
  }
  .bigFont{
     font-size:48px;
     font-weight:bold;
     color:#00ff00;
  }
</style>

<div id="div">Just keep doing every day.</div>
<input type="button" value="Change Font Class" onclick="changeFont()" />

<script type="text/javascript">

  function changeFont()
  {
     var div=document.getElementById("div");
     if(div.className=="smallFont")
     {
        div.className="bigFont";
     }
     else
     {
        div.className="smallFont";
     }
  }

</script>
```

CSS Overflow Expand and Close

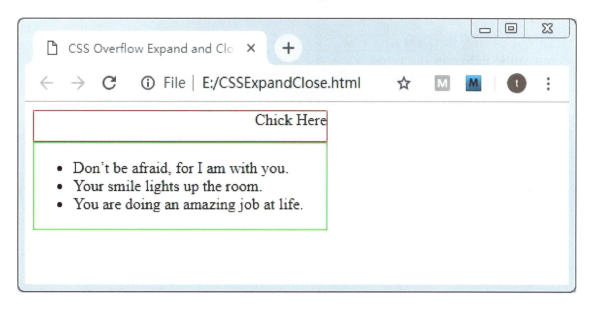

1. Create a CSSExpandClose.html file with Notepad and open it in your browser

```
<style type="text/css">
  .open{
    display :"" ;
  }

  .close{
    display :none ;
  }

  #div{
    width:300px;
    height:30px;
    border:1px solid #ff0000;
    text-align:right;
  }

  #div2{
    width:300px;
    border:1px solid #00ff00;
  }
</style>
```

```html
<div id="div" onclick="change()">Chick Here</div>
<div id="div2">
<ul>
  <li>Don't be afraid, for I am with you. </li>
  <li>Your smile lights up the room.</li>
  <li>You are doing an amazing job at life.</li>
</ul>
</div>

<script type="text/javascript">

  function change()
  {
     var div2=document.getElementById("div2");
     if(div2.className=="open")
     {
        div2.className="close";
     }
     else
     {
        div2.className="open";
     }
  }

</script>
```

CSS Floating Highlighting

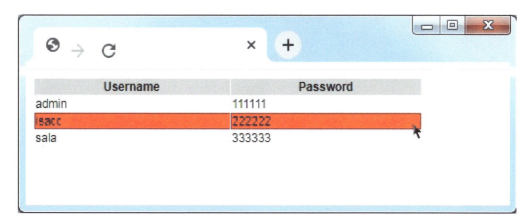

1. Create a CSSHighlighting.html file with Notepad and open it in your browser

```
<style type="text/css">
  .over{
    background-color: #ff0000;
  }

  .down{
    background-color: #0000ff;
  }

  table{
    border:1px solid #eeeeee;
    width:400px;
    border-collapse: collapse;
  }

  table th{
    border:1px solid #eeeeee;
    background-color: #cccccc;
  }

  table td{
    border:1px solid #eeeeee;
  }
</style>
```

```html
<table>
  <tr>
    <th>Username</th><th>Password</th>
  </tr>
  <tr onmousedown="doDown(this)" onmouseover="doOver(this)"
onmouseout="doOut(this)">
    <td>admin</td><td>111111</td>
  </tr>
  <tr onmousedown="doDown(this)"  onmouseover="doOver(this)"
onmouseout="doOut(this)">
    <td>isacc</td><td>222222</td>
  </tr>
  <tr onmousedown="doDown(this)"  onmouseover="doOver(this)"
onmouseout="doOut(this)">
    <td>sala</td><td>333333</td>
  </tr>
</table>

<script type="text/javascript">

  function doOver(obj){
    if(obj.className!="down"){
      obj.className="over";
    }
  }

  function doOut(obj){
    if(obj.className!="down"){
      obj.className="";
    }
  }

  function doDown(obj){
    if(obj.className!="down"){
      obj.className="down";
    }else{
      obj.className="over";
    }
  }

</script>
```

Table Create Rows Columns

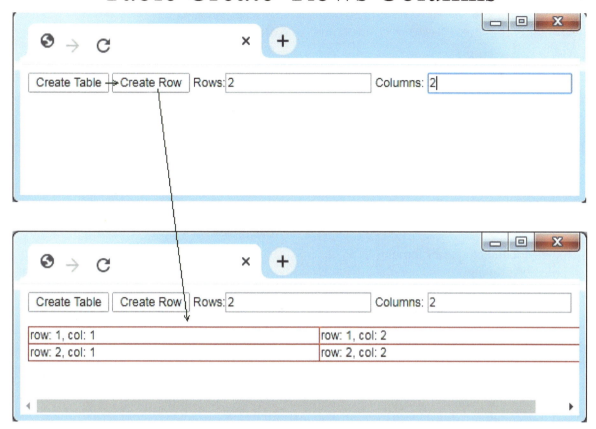

1. Create a TableCreate RowsColumns.html **file with** Notepad **and open it in your browser**

table.insertRow: inserts a new row (<tr>) in a given <table>, returns a reference to the new row.
table. insertCell: inserts a new col (<td>) in a given <tr>, returns a reference to the new col.

```
<style type="text/css">
  .tableClass{
    width:600px;
    border:1px solid #ff0000;
    border-collapse: collapse;
  }
  .tableClass td{
    border:1px solid #ff0000;
  }
</style>
```

```html
<input type="button" value="Create Table" onclick="doCreateTable()" />
<input type="button" value="Create Row" onclick="doCreateRow()" />
Rows:<input type="text" value="" id="row" /> Columns: <input type="text" value=""
id="col" />
<br>
<br>
<div id="div">

</div>

<script type="text/javascript">
    var table;
    function doCreateTable()
    {
        table=document.createElement("table");
        table.className="tableClass";

        document.getElementById("div").appendChild(table);
    }

    function doCreateRow()
    {
        var rowNum=parseInt(document.getElementById("row").value);
        var colNum=parseInt(document.getElementById("col").value);

        for(var i=1;i<=rowNum;i++)
        {
            var row=table.insertRow(-1);
            for(var j=1;j<=colNum;j++)
            {
                var cell=row.insertCell(-1);
                cell.innerHTML="row: "+i+", col: "+j;
            }
        }
    }

</script>
```

Delete Table Row Column

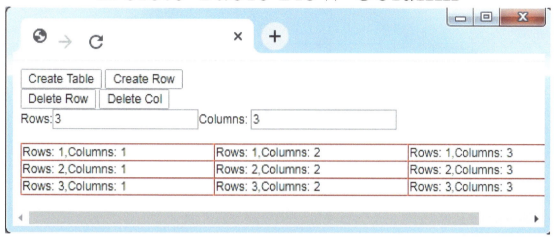

1. Create a DeleteTableRowColumn.html file with Notepad and open it in your browser

table. deleteCell: delete a cell in the current table row.

```
<style type="text/css">
  .tableClass{
    width:600px;
    border:1px solid #ff0000;
    border-collapse: collapse;
  }

  .tableClass td{
    border:1px solid #ff0000;
  }
</style>
<input type="button" value="Create Table" onclick="doCreateTable()" />
<input type="button" value="Create Row" onclick="doCreateRow()" />
<br>
<input type="button" value="Delete Row" onclick="doDeleteRow()" />
<input type="button" value="Delete Col" onclick="doDeleteCol()" />
<br>
Rows:<input type="text" value="" id="row" />Columns: <input type="text" value=""
id="col" />
<br>
<br>
<div id="div"> </div>
```

```
<script type="text/javascript">
    var table;
    function doCreateTable()
    {
        table=document.createElement("table");
        table.className="tableClass";
        document.getElementById("div").appendChild(table);
    }

    function doCreateRow()
    {
        var rowNum=parseInt(document.getElementById("row").value);
        var colNum=parseInt(document.getElementById("col").value);

        for(var i=1;i<=rowNum;i++)
        {
            var row=table.insertRow(-1);
            for(var j=1;j<=colNum;j++)
            {
                var cell=row.insertCell(-1);
                cell.innerHTML="Rows: "+i+",Columns: "+j;
            }
        }
    }


    function doDeleteRow()
    {
        var rowNum=parseInt(document.getElementById("row").value);
        table.deleteRow(rowNum);
    }

    function doDeleteCol()
    {
        var colNum=parseInt(document.getElementById("col").value);
        var rows=table.rows;
        for(var i=0;i<rows.length;i++)
        {
            rows[i].deleteCell(colNum);
        }
    }
</script>
```

Timer

1. Create a Timer.html file with Notepad and open it in your browser

getFullYear():   Get the year as a four digit number (yyyy)
getMonth():   Get the month as a number (0-11)
getDate():   Get the day as a number (1-31)
getHours():   Get the hour (0-23)
getMinutes():   Get the minute (0-59)
getSeconds():   Get the second (0-59)
getTime():   Get the time (milliseconds since January 1, 1970)
setInterval():   continue calling the function until clearInterval() is called.

```
<div id="dateDiv" ></div>

<script type="text/javascript">
  function doSetInterval()
  {
     var dateDiv=document.getElementById("dateDiv");
     var d=new Date();
     var dateString = d.getHours()+":"+d.getMinutes()+":"+d.getSeconds()

     dateDiv.innerHTML=dateString;
  }

  setInterval("doSetInterval()",1000);
</script>
```

Thanks for learning, if you want to learn web coding, please study book

https://www.amazon.com/dp/B086PVSKTN

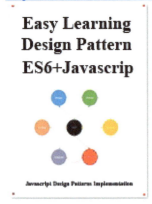

https://www.amazon.com/dp/B08D4Y5454

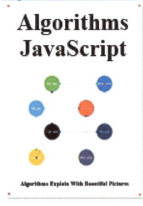

If you enjoyed this book and found some benefit in reading this, I'd like to hear from you and hope that you could take some time to post a review on Amazon. Your feedback and support will help us to greatly improve in future and make this book even better.

You can follow this link now.

http://www.amazon.com/review/create-review?&asin=1078285233

Different country reviews only need to modify the amazon domain name in the link:
www.amazon.co.uk
www.amazon.de
www.amazon.fr
www.amazon.es
www.amazon.it
www.amazon.ca
www.amazon.nl
www.amazon.in
www.amazon.co.jp
www.amazon.com.br
www.amazon.com.mx
www.amazon.com.au

I wish you all the best in your future success!

www.ingramcontent.com/pod-product-compliance
Lightning Source LLC
Chambersburg PA
CBHW041427050326
40689CB00003B/685